lisa frank

GIANT Sticker Activity Book

DIRECTIONS:

LOOK FOR STICKERS THAT FIT THE COLORED SHAPES FOUND THROUGHOUT THIS BOOK.

THE SHEETS INCLUDE BONUS STICKERS THAT CAN BE USED WITH THE FUN ACTIVITIES OR USE THEM TO MAKE YOUR OWN PICTURES!

THIS BOOK BELONGS TO:

©2012
Bendon Publishing Int'l, Inc.
Ashland, OH 44805
www.bendonpub.com

Cassie
Surfer Girl

Where She Lives: Cassie®, the super surfin' sweetie, lives near a famous Fantastic World® beach that's renowned for it's awesome waves. She lives with her little surfing pal, a Chihuahua named Cameo®; they make quite a sensation.

Where You Will Find Her: Always on her surfboard, she's staking out the beaches, looking for the perfect waves. When she's not 'hanging ten', she loves to just float in the lagoon, hanging out with Cameo® and her dolphin friend, Marina®.

Personality: Cassie® is fearless in the water, some think she's part mermaid! And out of the water, she is just as bold! Not just her personality, but also her style! Her passion for fashion is almost as big as her passion for smashin' the waves!

Likes: Any water sports, shopping, designing her own surfboards and swim suits, letting Cameo® ride on her board and baking coconut cream pie (which she shares with Cameo® and Marina®!).

Dislikes: Plastic, hungry sharks, licorice, rip tides.

Memorable Quotes: "Chihuahuabunga!", "Go for it!...You've got to get your feet wet, before you can ride the waves!", "It's good to make a splash!"

Use your bonus stickers to finish the picture

IMAGE SCRAMBLE

CAREFULLY REMOVE THE PUZZLE PIECES ON THE STICKER PAGE AND
PLACE THEM ON THE SQUARE WITH THE MATCHING LETTER OR NUMBER ON THE GRID.

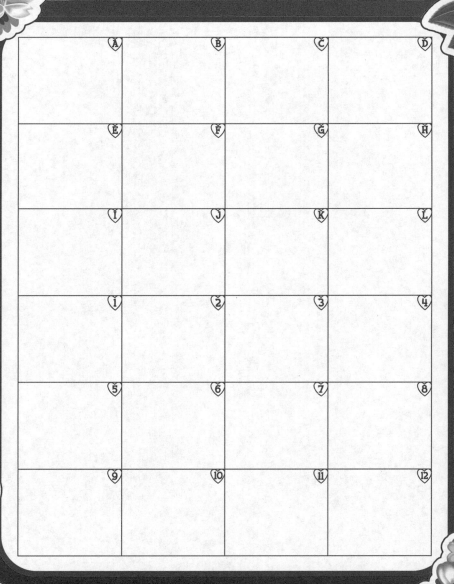

WORD SEARCH

FIND AND CIRCLE THE WORDS IN THE PUZZLE BELOW.

BUTTERFLY

FLAMINGO

TURTLE

DRAGONFLY

RAINBOW

WATERMELON

CROWN

LADYBUG

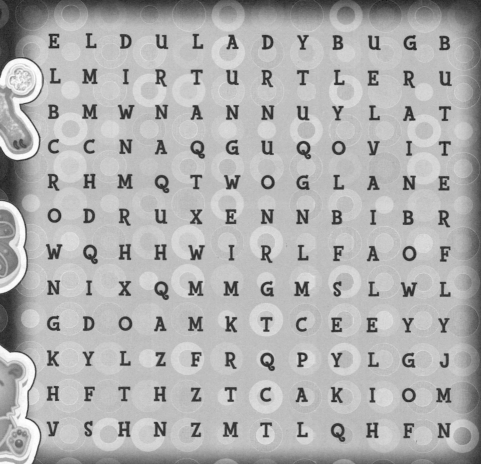

```
E L D U L A D Y B U G B
L M I R T U R T L E R U
B M W N A N N U Y L A T
C C N A Q G U Q O V I T
R H M Q T W O G L A N E
O D R U X E N N B I B R
W Q H H W I R L F A O F
N I X Q M M G M S L W L
G D O A M K T C E E Y Y
K Y L Z F R Q P Y L G J
H F T H Z T C A K I O M
V S H N Z M T L Q H F N
```

MATCHING CLOSE UP

MATCH THE CHARACTERS BY WRITING THE
CORRECT LETTER BELOW EACH CLOSE-UP.

A   B   C

1   2   3

4   5   6

CRACK THE CODE

SHHHH...TATEY BUG® HAS A SECRET SHE WANTS TO SHARE
ONLY WITH YOU. USING THE SECRET CODE BELOW, FILL
IN THE BLANKS AND REVEAL THE HIDDEN WORDS!

A	B	C	D	E	F	G	H	I

J	K	L	M	N	O	P	Q	R

S	T	U	V	W	X	Y	Z

ANSWER: SHE CAN FLY!

NOW THAT YOU HAVE TATEY BUG®'S SECRET CODE,
TRY MAKING YOUR OWN SECRET MESSAGE.

7

WORD MAZE

TRAVEL THROUGH THE MAZE TO HELP HIPPIE GIRL GET TO THE PEACE SIGN IN THE CENTER. YOU CAN ONLY PASS THROUGH OPENINGS THAT SPELL THE WORD "PEACE" IN ORDER.

START

FINISH

8

TRANSFER

USING THE PATHS, TRANSFER THE LETTERS INTO THE BOXES TO UNSCRAMBLE THE WORDS

Tikanni

Where He Lives: Tikanni™ lives in the land of Northern Lights, where the rainbow dances in the evening sky and glittering snowflakes dazzle the landscape!

Where You'll Find Him: Tikanni™ spends his days playing in the snow with his polar pals, husk-skiing down the massive snow drifts or ice skating, which in doggy terms means sliding across the ice on his nicely padded paws-terior.

Personality: Hardy and adventurous, Tikanni™ doesn't get snowdays, since everyday is a snowday! He loves the frosty cold temperatures which makes him one cool canine!

Likes: Digging snow caves, extreme weather sports, catchingsnowflakes, his favorite food is penguinnie linguine– a northernspecialty perfected by his penguin friends.

Dislikes: Thin ice, frost bite, palm trees (saw a picture once and thought they were the weirdest trees he had ever seen!)

Favorite Games: Snarf a Snowball and Tag the Penguin

Memorable Quotes: "I would never bite Jack Frost!"

Use your bonus stickers to finish the picture.

11

HOW MANY WORDS

HOW MANY WORDS CAN YOU MAKE USING THE LETTERS IN

Jolie-Marie

EXAMPLE: EMAIL

PARTY MAZE

MATCH THE STICKERS TO THE MISSING SHAPES IN THE MAZE. WHEN THE MAZE IS COMPLETE, HELP HOLLYWOOD BEAR™ FIND HIS WAY THE THE PARTY.

Rainbow Chaser & Lollipop

A lush grassy pasture in the Fantastic World of Lisa Frank (Magicful Meadow), -corral, ranch, secret pond.

Personality: Loves to laugh, gentle, very thoughtful, introspective, shy.

Long Term Goal: To become a race horse.

Hobbies: Day dreaming, running, dancing is her secret talent- she practices her fancy footwork at night.

Smelling Fragrant flowers, eating sweet apples feeling the wind whip through her mane.

Bees, rainy days, feeling left out, show-offs.

Where You Will Find Lollipop: Any where her big sister is.

Personality: She is very curious and pesters Rainbow Chaser constantly for answers to her questions. Her curiousity can sometimes get her in trouble, and occasionally she can be found horsing around, but she is usually a very well behaved little pony!

Likes: Discovering something new, going for long walks and eatting anything with lots of sugar!

Dislikes: Bedtime, when Rainbow Chaser says "Just because" to one of her questions.

14

RAINBOW-TAC-TOE

USE YOUR STICKERS AND CHALLENGE A FRIEND TO A FUN GAME OF TIC-TAC-TOE!

GAME #1

GAME #2

GAME #3

GAME #4

TULIP TROUBLE

A MIX-UP AT THE FLOWER SHOP HAS LEFT THEM WITH TOO MANY TULIPS. CAN YOU FIND THE CORRECT BEAUTIFUL BOUQUET? MATCH THE STICKERS TO THE RELATED COORDINATES ON THE GRID. THEN USE THE CLUES BELOW TO REVEAL THE ANSWER.

CLUE 1: THERE IS ONLY 1 YELLOW TULIP

CLUE 2: THE VASE HAS BLUE IN IT

CLUE 3: THE MIDDLE FLOWER IS NOT PINK

CLUE 4: THE VASE IS MORE THAN ONE COLOR

Tatey Bug

Where she lives: Tatey Bug® lives in the Flowerful Forest, a very special and magical part of the Fantastic World of Lisa Frank®. Her forest is filled not just with flowers, but all kinds of feathery and fluffy friends!

Where you will find her: Tatey Bug® spends time exploring the forest, finding new friends and playing with all the cute and cuddly creatures that live there. She doesn't have to look to hard to find her little forest friends because she has such a kind heart, all the animals find her!

Personality: Smart, artistic, curious and compassionate. Tatey Bug® has a knack for finding those in need. She is also passionate about tending her flowers, that make the forest a magical spectacle for all who visit!

Likes: All animals, sunshine, gardening, exploring and hiking, flying (one of her secrets)...shhhhh! Ladybugs (of course), and anything with honey.

Dislikes: Bullies

Memorable Quotes:

"Magic lives within every creature!"

Use your bonus stickers
to finish the picture.

HOW MANY WORDS

HOW MANY WORDS CAN YOU MAKE USING THE LETTERS IN

Rainbow MATINEE™

EXAMPLE: REMOTE

WHO IS WHO

DRAW A LINE TO MATCH THE CHARACTERS TO THEIR NAMES.

Purrscilla

Cassie Surfer Girl

Dancing Dolphins

21

IMAGE SCRAMBLE

CAREFULLY REMOVE THE PUZZLE PIECES ON THE STICKER PAGE AND
PLACE THEM ON THE SQUARE WITH THE MATCHING LETTER OR NUMBER ON THE GRID.

SECRET MESSAGE

CROSS OUT THE WORD **HUNTER** EVERY TIME YOU SEE IT IN THE BOX. WHEN YOU REACH A LETTER THAT DOES NOT BELONG, WRITE IT IN THE CIRCLES BELOW TO REVEAL THE SECRET MESSAGE.

```
HUNTERTHUNTERHHUNTEREH
UNTERRHUNTEREHUNTERIHU
NTERSHUNTERNHUNTEREHUN
TERVHUNTEREHUNTERRHUNT
ERAHUNTERDHUNTERUHUNTE
RLHUNTERLHUNTERMHUNTER
OHUNTERMHUNTEREHUNTER
NHUNTERTHUNTERWHUNTERI
HUNTERTHUNTERHHUNTERH
HUNTERIHUNTERMHUNTERAH
UNTERRHUNTEROHUNTERUH
UNTERNHUNTERDHUNTER
```

(Secret message: THERE IS NEVER A DULL MOMENT WITH HIM AROUND!)

23

Purrscilla®

Where She Lives: In a plush penthouse atop the colorful city lights of the Fantastic World of Lisa Frank®.

Where You Will Find Her: Her daily routine includes lounging upon her cushy kitty bed, going to the salon where she is brushed and puffed into a ball of silky fluff, and purrhaps a stop at her favorite bling shop!

Likes: Colorful nail pawlish, anything that sparkles, 'penthouse perching' (a pastime that involves sitting in the window, watching all the city activity below), lobster kabobs with cream sauce, fine art.

Dislikes: Canned tuna, sirens or other loud obnoxious noises, humidity.

"A posh pillow is the key to a purrfect cat-nap!", "Anything is posh-able!", "Pampering is for pussycats!"

Use your stickers to decorate Purrscilla®.

WORD SCRAMBLE

USING THE WORDS FROM THE LIST, UNSCRAMBLE THE
LETTERS TO CORRECTLY SPELL THE NAMES AND WORDS.

USEPR _____

TILSKPIC _____

GSASULSNES _____

ECALKCEN _____

TRECALEB _____

PRETTY PUZZLE

CAREFULLY REMOVE THE PUZZLE PIECES ON THE STICKER PAGE
AND PLACE THEM ON THE MATCHING SHAPE ON THE GRID

MISSING PIECE

FIND THE MISSING PIECE OF THE IMAGE, THEN USE
THE MATCHING STICKER TO FINISH THE PICTURE!

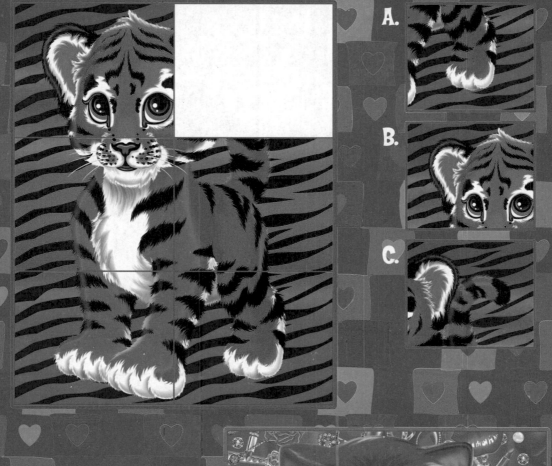

A.

B.

C.

D.

E.

F.

THERE ARE MANY GREAT FRIENDS TO FIND IN THE WONDERFUL
WORLD OF LISA FRANK! THESE ARE PHOTOS OF SOME OF THEM.
USE YOUR STICKERS TO FINISH THE PICTURES.

29

SQUARES

TWO PLAYERS TAKE TURNS, DRAWING A LINE FROM ONE CUPECAKE TO ANOTHER. WHOEVER MAKES THE LINE THAT COMPLETES THE BOX PUTS THEIR STICKER FROM THE CORRESPONDING STICKER SHEET INSIDE THAT BOX. THE PERSON WITH THE MOST SQUARES AT THE END OF THE GAME WINS!

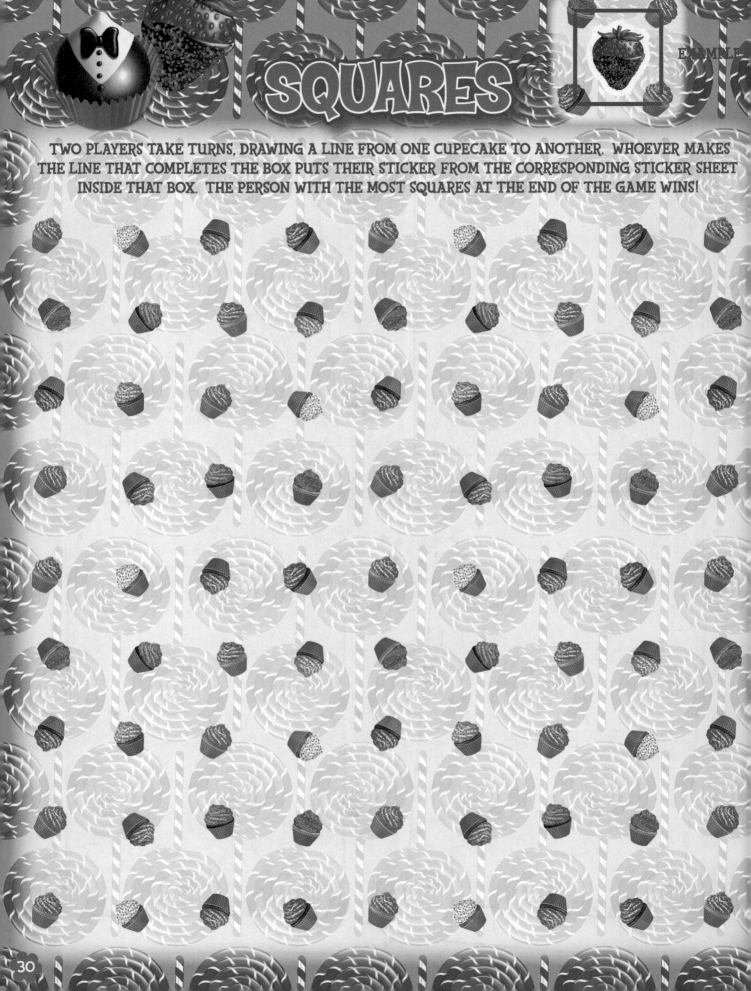

CROSSED WORDS

USING THE WORDS FROM THE WORD LIST
COMPLETE THIS INTERLOCKED WORD PUZZLE

31

Rainbow MAJESTY

Where She Lives: Rainbow Majesty lives in the mystical land beyond the rainbow and among the stars, where the colors are so brilliant it has to be part of the Fantastic World of Lisa Frank!

Where You Will Find Her: Rainbow Majesty spends her days prancing, princessing and color seeking. The rainbow has turned her mane into a mass of colorful curls that she loves to keep braided and bedazzled!

Personality: Rainbow Majesty rules the rainbow realm. Even though she is confident, proud and royally ravishing, she has a bashful smile and humble spirit.

Likes: Brilliant colors, anything sweet, jewels, star gazing, getting her mane styled.

Dislikes: Gray, smoke, and being cooped up.

Memorable Quotes: "Every color of the rainbow is a treasure beyond all measure."

Use your stickers to decorate Rainbow Majesty.

Stickers for page 1

Stickers for page 2

Stickers for pages 4 & 5

Stickers for pages 6 & 7

More stickers for pages 6 & 7

Stickers for page 8

Stickers for page 9

Stickers for page 10

Stickers for
page 12

Tikanni

Stickers for page 13

Stickers for page 14

Stickers for page 16

Rainbow Chaser™ & Lollipop™

Stickers for page 16 ♡

Stickers for page 17

C4 B1 A2

A3 B4 C2

A1 A4 C3

B2 B3 C1

Stickers for page 18

Stickers for page 20

Stickers for page 21

Cassie Surfer Girl

Stickers for page 21

More stickers for pages 22 & 23

Stickers for page 24

Purrscilla

Dancing Dolphins

Purrscilla

More stickers for page 24

Stickers for page 25

BRACELET

PURSE

LIPSTICK

NECKLACE

SUNGLASSES

More stickers for page 26

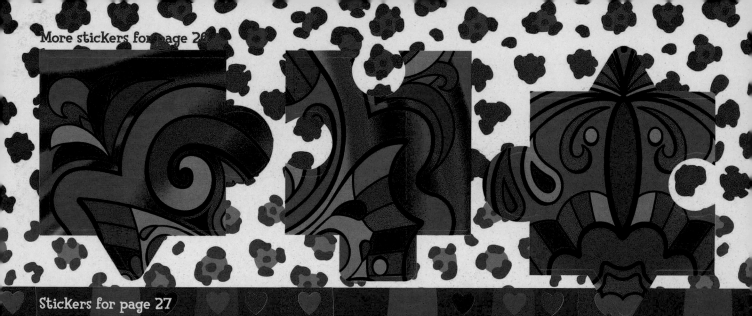

More stickers for page 26

Stickers for page 27

A.

B.

C.

D.

E.

F.

Stickers for pages 28 & 29

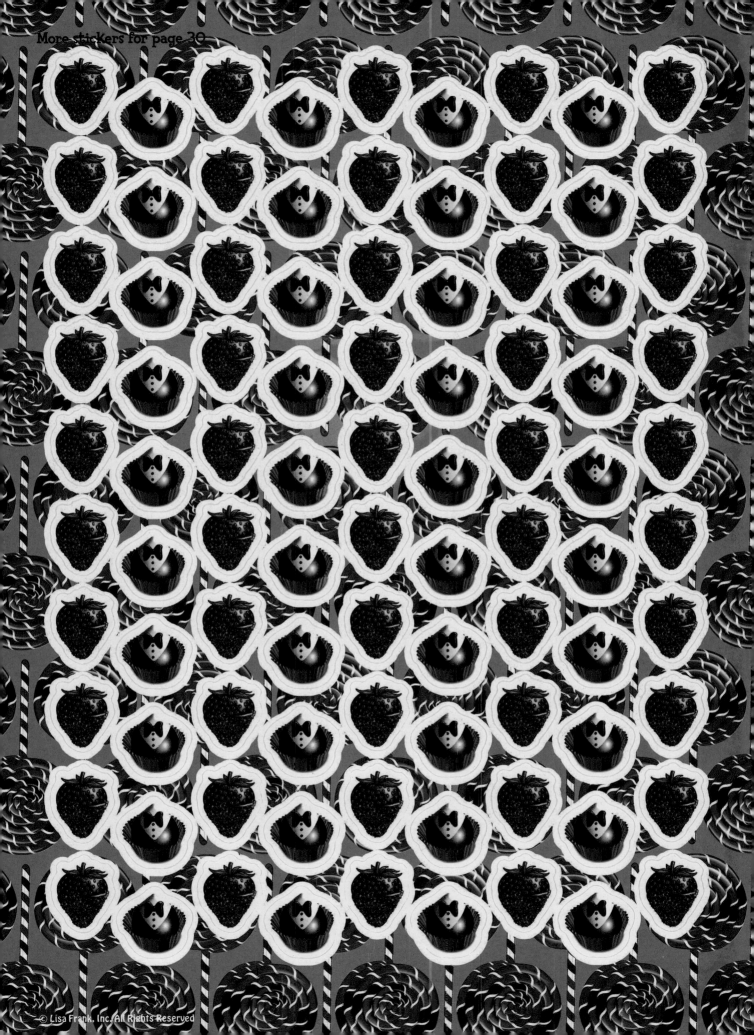

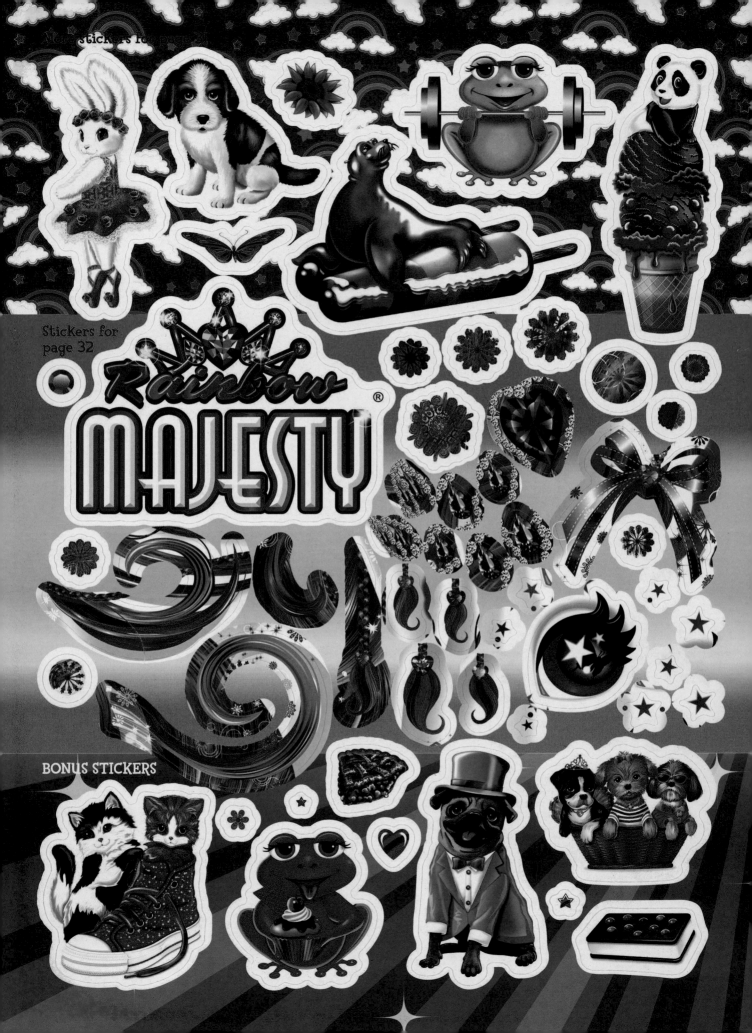

Stickers for
page 32

Rainbow
MAJESTY ®

BONUS STICKERS

BONUS STICKERS

BONUS STICKERS

BONUS STICKERS